GW00727875

ABOUT THE AUTHOR

Mireille Saba Redford was born in Beirut before moving to Sydney where she worked as an interpreter and a newspaper editor and wrote poetry and short stories which granted her an award at The Sydney Writers' Festival. She has four publications including *The Anthology of Contemporary Australian Poetry*.

Redford is a university professor and a college co-ordinator in Beirut. She established two poetry magazines in English and is a proven team-leader encouraging excellence in performance. She has recently been named as "one of the best poets of the century" by *STARS Illustrated* magazine – New York Press.

DEDICATION

To you, Dad.

To you, Chris.

And to the One who's out there…

Mireille Saba Redford

A WORLD
OF STONE

New and Selected Poems

AUSTIN MACAULEY PUBLISHERS™

LONDON • CAMBRIDGE • NEW YORK • SHARJAH

Copyright © Mireille Saba Redford (2021)

The right of Mireille Saba Redford to be identified as author of this work has been asserted in accordance with section 77 and 78 of the Copyright, Designs and Patents Act 1988.

All rights reserved. No part of this publication may be reproduced, stored in a retrieval system, or transmitted in any form or by any means, electronic, mechanical, photocopying, recording, or otherwise, without the prior permission of the publishers.

Any person who commits any unauthorised act in relation to this publication may be liable to criminal prosecution and civil claims for damages.

Cover painting by Juliano Habib.

A CIP catalogue record for this title is available from the British Library.

ISBN 9781528984270 (Paperback)
ISBN 9781528984287 (Hardback)
ISBN 9781528984294 (ePub e-book)

www.austinmacauley.com

First Published (2021)
Austin Macauley Publishers Ltd
25 Canada Square
Canary Wharf
London
E14 5LQ

ACKNOWLEDGEMENTS

Writing a poetry book has not been an easy task amidst the hustle and bustle of daily commitments. But none of this would have been possible without the people who have walked into my life, whether temporarily or permanently, but kept me going.

I am eternally grateful to my son, Christopher, who gave me all the heavenly blessings a mother would dream of. To all my family members who have been so supportive of my work and taught me love, values and respect, especially my father figure, Father Saba who has been the person I could turn to during my desperate moments. And to my little nephews and nieces: Alessandro, Ivan, Tracy and Jacky who filled my life with joy, and whose dreams I strive to turn into realities.

I would also like to thank my amazing bosses and co-workers who stood by me and helped me succeed.

I am also forever thankful to my friends in Beirut who have been a true inspiration to me. I am forever indebted to them! And I owe all my gratitude to my far away folks in Sydney who made all my ups and downs in life an easy bridge to cross.

A very special thanks to the editors who worked on the book production, and the publishing team at Austin Macauley. Thank you!

POEMS

My Child

And I look at you, first
With unspoken white words
Your eyes nearing paradise
Will eternity suffice?

Precious heart, precious soul
Precious dew
Your days are now rolling
Fresh and new.

And my mind tells me a million stories:

"In the past time bubble
There was a small child
Who played in the big puddle
And loved to be wild.

A child of this world
From his sleep he emerged
Who enjoyed to be cuddled
And enough love to have piled.

He quickly learned his ABC
From A to Z
His music was louder
And his sun much brighter.

He made great booby traps
And drove his cars fast to crash
He liked flinging his trucks
And with every chance shot the pucks.

He spent hours on animated cartoons
Querying about serious matters in depth
He made things disappear in magic tricks
Boasting proudly about his little strength."

How can distance make you mild
Towards the wind flow unbound?
My deep scar! Can you feel?
With your hand, can you heal?

Upside-Down

Fancy yourself waking up
And feeling turned upside-down

Holding a mighty blade, not a cup
And stabbing yourself till you drown.

Your mind is out of kilter
Feeling hard to recover

And your body a convicted bolter
Hiding in back alleys like a hater.

Transforming suddenly into Gregor Samsa
Unable to display your virtuoso.

Struggling with an insane intruder
Becoming inexplicably nuder

Awaiting a menacing disaster
Making the devil your solo master.

Fancy yourself running around
And the world on a time countdown

Then a few more minutes of stopover
Before everything turns lively over.

The New Unicorn

Fancy an old mythical unicorn
With its flowing mane and sparkling horn

Of super power and magic strength
Travelling the distance in great depth

With all the king's horses and all the king's men
Failing to uproot its alluring mane.

This great myth once planted intense fears
Before a new unicorn appears

Filled with fluffy sexual lust
Defying our flaming trust.

This skull-crusher would not break off nor cease
To put the kibosh on our release

Behaving like a stray animal
Or more like an artful cannibal.

This coiffed new-fashioned unicorn
Is conspicuously now reborn

Pressing his polished restart
To break all humans apart.

The Grey of Life

I walk inside not knowing what I would find
A long time has elapsed, gotten out of mind.

Walls split and cracked, time hasn't been so kind.
I couldn't stand the fall but I've to bind.

Without its doors, windows, let alone frames
As if the house had been rampaged by flames.

Weeds growing in and out of deep fissures
In my veins, which bleed at their apertures.

The flow is of darkest colour one could ever imagine
Abhorrence has given the place a deadly injection.

Rubble and silts reveal long years of deposits
For gnomes and what is left of the earth's treasures.

Cold and lifeless voices in their sleep tied
Speak from their world: "*Nobody lives inside!*"

No army in the world could protect your border
During the promise of peace or at times of war.

The farm which you inherited under the blue skies
Built on a solid mountain in a green paradise

Where gardens boomed and bloomed and grew
Had brought you misery when space blew.

In the distance, carpenter ants slide inside their hole
And a flower stretches shyly as if to console.

Years of fractional discord and perpetual strife
Leave a bitter after-taste of the grey of life

A neutral tone between black and white
Makes you slip away even when you're right.

The deplorable plight of the living and the dead
Succumbs to the reality you long to dread.

Gone but your souls have kept their identity
The buds of light, flowers of serenity.

Desire which once burned fiercely in your hearts
This warm radiance of no surrender, it reignites.

My Genome

My clock is running out
Symptoms are lingering.
Lustrous things are changing
In my own flesh and blood.

Sitting on an ancient megalith
Gazing at my inner labyrinth
Heart slain by straight arrows
Drowning in bleeding sorrows.

Where has all this led to?

More than twenty thousand genes
Pile in on supposedly clean chromosomes
Which I can't modify by any means
But can more easily heave stones.

A unique line of characteristics
Luckily, with no genetic disorder.
No biology, chemistry or physics
Has perfectly ticked in order.

Years have passed, fortunately
With minor mishaps and delay.
But the undying tides of history
Are being slowly washed away.

A World of Stone

Black, white and yellow
Muslim, Jew and Christian
African, Chinese and American
In a utensil supposedly mellow.

A barrel where justice is prevalent
Yet it seems to be intolerant.
Less amiable, more dominant
More hateful, less pleasant.

This world is for the fits
For the lords and the kings
For agony and extremism
Not for tolerance and altruism.

This world is for science
For death installed in a machine.
For the universal reliance
And drugs with the suffix -ine.

Slaves of this god
Pay him tribute
To stay enchained
In the realm of solitude.

A destructive yet destructible force
There is no time for remorse
To even catch our own breath
Detestation of the mind and death.

This world is not for poets
Nor for talented painters
Creative choreographers
And born philosophers.

A fragmented world
For dynamos and aminos
For thinkers and astronomers
And the ruling underworld.

Daily Testers

These kempt daily testers
Leave us dying of thirst
Throw us into the pits
Feeling about to burst.

Banging our heads against a brick wall
Like oxen being ruthlessly slaughtered.
Watching every step as not to fall
Entangled and never rewarded.

Forced to believe money is poisonous
Tricked into buying digital instead.
Criticism is considered treasonous
Though we know we're being beastly misled.

It was supposed to be about democracy
Shifting the focus from bad corruption.
Now it's become a total cacophony.
Who could explain this contradiction?

Keeping our wits about us
Locked in a greenhouse effect.
Don't dare make a plea or a fuss
Even when all around is wrecked.

These testers are intricate plots
Capturing us without being captured.
Conspire to overpower us
Making us morally corrupt.

Love or hate, both are the same.
Our acts are irremediable.
Wondering who would take the blame
Wounds can seldom be treatable.

Haunted by our past buried in a coffin
Like a vessel that had left its berth.
Up the stream, migrating salmon are drawn in
Sustaining life from the moment of birth.

A Cold Day in Hell

The old Christian mortalism
Speaks of the 'must die' doctrine.

The 'blessed' are saved
The 'wicked' destroyed

As stated by Saint Patrick's purgatory
That determines a soul's suitability.

To justify this hazy distinction
We have given it a new dimension.

The gate has mortal gatekeepers
Commanding like its sole judges

Torn between agony or pleasure
Wiping out the monastic order.

Once the land of great religions
Now inhabited by demons.

Evil lords have no divine pardon.
Rivers of blood wash out the fearsome.

Blasphemous souls and prostrate sinners
Inflict pain on the wise believers.

Poor burials for ardent devotees
To be welcomed into heavenly fields.

Devourers failing purification
Are thrown straight into annihilation.

The penal code strikes great numbers of beings
In accordance with their heinous misdeeds.

Gloomy place of anguish and torment
Where torture is the first commandment.

Hellish components lie in various chambers.
See no paradise despite their penitence.

Our guides through heaven and inferno
Grant us no escape when confined to Limbo.

No book of genesis or Revelation
Supreme deity or eternal salvation

Says we shall not escape condemnation
Or our souls shall burn for damnation.

Corruption of the human race
Despite the good-god on its face.

Dead souls can never be heard
What's gotten into the world?

Fast turning into steel
Wasted, don't try to heal.

Citizens of Our Own

Cells, cells, and cells…
So they say our cells
Are a country of 10,000 trillion citizens.
Each a complete organism in itself
Devoted to a specialised self
To keep our overall well-being on a shelf.

Cells, cells, and cells…
The oldest building blocks
And yet the most perfect baulks
Banding together in docks
Forming tissues, bones and organs
To give a myriad of proportions.

A fundamental molecule of life
Operating as an independent unit.
Able to replicate itself, divide
Swim, reproduce, unite
Grow, manufacture, connect
Change, control, protect
Operate, prevent, regenerate
And to our mind, migrate.

Cells, cells, and cells…
Why can't we just adjust
To be like you inside of us?
Barely eight billion inhabitants
On a killing-spree hunt
A war zone and a battlefront
We find it hard to live as one nation.
What a miserable shameful dysfunction!

A so-called harmonious world
Curled, swirled and twirled.
Fights, wars and hunger
And death taking a little bit longer.
With top first-class world citizens
Unable to lead, conjoin and prevent,
The place is heavily loaded with carcinogens
Burying us daily under deep cement.

Tell Me, Pa!

I close my eyes
A glimpse of heaven living.

Tell me, Pa!
What do you see up there?

Do you see clouds and rain?
Do you see the Good Shepherd, sain?

Is there immense intensity
Intense immensity

One true force to foreordain
Immortal values to retain

United plurality
Boundless charity

No wind or hurricane
A sacred breath to sustain

Perhaps natural tranquillity
Or infinite equality

An everlasting entity
Perhaps one real identity?

Tell me, Pa!

Immortal souls all-embracing
Do they share the same craving?

Striving towards the infinite
Is their stay indefinite?

Is heaven really white
Is there no place for the night?

Are you profoundly at peace?
And the truth, did you seize?

Tell me what do you see
Is eternal light truly a glee?

Self-Condemnation

On a deserted road
Strewn with dust load
Sand, dirt and bone
I travel alone.

The Utopian world I once sought
With danger it is fraught.
A defeated raging animal
A wild zone sadly abysmal.

My mind contemplates
Some failures and regrets.
Hitherto a quasi-union
And taboos not to mention:

Dreams I've longed to keep
But had unfulfilled.

Eyes I've yearned to capture
But found dispersed.

Cries I've wanted to release
But carried unleashed.

Gaps I've yearned to fill
But left unfilled.

Moments I would've died to freeze
But seen all drenched.
Words I've longed to speak
But left unspoken.

Now, alone and in chain
With a bad case of shakes
Sudden twinges of pain
And hard chronic aches.

Regrets not yet over
For missed opportunities
And past mistakes
Weighing on a heavy bender.

Tears are gushing in vain
Down this narrow lane
And deep infinite affection
For a timeless reunion.

Imperishable moments
In perishable thoughts
Dragged in ailments
Coming down to naught.

Flesh all flaked
On a wounded horse
With ageing remorse
Worn-out and quaked.

Time Machine

You think you can beat time
And make each day a prime.
Think you can control its mind
From the front and from behind.

The time machine is moving
At a steady pace cruising.

Near or far
Slow or fast

Stepping on everything
Leaving you without wings

Grinding you into powder
Watching you weep louder

Melting your minds and your souls
Throwing you into deep holes

Your dreams proving to be ephemeral
And your vision only peripheral

Taking you on a wicked witch hunt
Sending your troops to guard the front

Spinning you on a roundabout
Then ruthlessly spitting you out.

Make Me Love You

Make me love you the way greatest lovers did
In unique stories sought after by avid.

Like Juliet, Guinevere and Francesca
Isolde, Eurydice and Cleopatra.

Mastership of the rarest love and intensity
Beauty which can never doubt its reachability.

Make me the one star of all your nights
Consumed by the pursuit of my flights.

Make me the nymph of all your virtues
Falling in love with your charming blues.

Take me on this everlasting ride
Swing me with the movements of the tide

Perhaps where things recover at a slow interval
A tale of hope and ardour that assures survival.

Make us embark on a tale against all odds
Indulge the divine nature like two small tods

Submerge in the capsule of our genuine feelings
Devour the harsh reality without human achings.

Stride through more peaks created in history
Devote more space to our neutral territory

Gain the power to subjugate obsessive fun
Loathing, resentment and aversion to shun.

Tell me how complicated the situation is
But let each and every moment in time freeze.

The waterfalls will remain our attraction
Coming home tomorrow is now an assumption.

I truly yearn and yearn for this futuristic stride
For both of our solemn souls have already died.

It All Started

It all started with

Ultraviolet and infrared
Before colours were lively widespread.

Stars and planets were there, too
Before Man certainly grew.

Then it all started again with you
Before you raged, boiled and badly blew.

Your whole life hanging by a thread
A truth you gushed out with mere dread.

Committing all the misdeed
Ignoring all those in need

Believing that stardom
Was reserved to officialdom

Abducting and murdering
Trafficking and slaughtering

Making lives lay waste and ravaged
With their trust forever damaged.

Free delivery straight to your door
Making the wealthy rapidly poor.

If this is your way of justice
It is truly a death notice.

Or your idea of perfection
You'd better uphold their conviction

Until the picture is redrawn
For the onset of a new dawn.

If There Is Tomorrow

If there is tomorrow
Words would no longer falter
Values would never alter
And earth would be an altar.

Stones would breathe life
Same as trees strive.
Borders would suddenly disappear
And families prosper year after year.

We'd ask snow to fall
And it'd fall.
And the sun to shine
And it'd shine.

We'd say to the mountain: move
And it'd move.
To the fig: die
And it'd die.

If there's tomorrow
Spirits from above and below
Would sing the melody of earth
Without cursing at their own birth.

One virtuous power filling all
Winter, spring, summer and even fall
Beginning and end with inclusions
To sum up all of the conclusions.

To Protect and Serve

Sirens wailing
Boys shooting
A girl overdosing
Heads not turning.

Down the other street
You'd better walk discreet.
One could feel intense heat
For another heart won't beat.

Back alleys become crowded
Guns are firing powder
Cries are getting louder
And moms no longer prouder.

Another body gone to waste
With a gunshot in his chest.
The police made an arrest
A crime too hard to digest.

He was just another teen
With big ambitions and a dream.
But owed 'em money for a deal
Murder, rape and steal.

A piece of sky just fell
And got mixed in real hell.
People aren't feeling well.
It's time to say farewell.

You've got to pay the debt
Or consider it a threat.
Sign your death certificate
Hoping to find your DNA dragnet.

"Dear, Policeman
Call me god!
Catch me if you can
I'm not that odd.

I have a list of people to die later
I hunt and kill like a gator
I'm one of those hard cases
And not on your databases."

Those who do others harm
Treat 'em like cattle on a farm.
They don't care about wasted charm
Instead of living arm in arm.

What a job, what a mess!
Is this progress or regress?
Wearing black in distress
It's high time to confess.

To protect and to serve
You'll have to have the nerve.
Justice you'll need to preserve.
Bigger than a medal you deserve.

Magic Mirror

- Magic mirror
Speak louder!

Who's the most beautiful girl
In the world?

"Not you, my dear
I say, not out of fear.

In a moment spurred
Beauty is blurred."

- Who's the most charming man
In the world?

"He was never here
Wasn't it obvious and clear?"

- Who's the most powerful person
In the world?

"The ones who tortures
All across the borders."

- Magic mirror
Who's then humane?

"Don't search in vain.
Call it a loss, not a gain."

- Magic mirror
Can the sky be blue?

"Even if it seems so
It tastes like sorrow!"

- Magic mirror
Ugly terror!

A Moment of Humanity

Strange swamp creatures
Roam the spaces
Seemingly good
Devilishly bad
Fighting one another
With no regard or moral.

Kill the natives
Kill the blacks
Kill the whites
Kill the addicts
Kill the women
Kill the teens.

"I was here first," says one.
"I am here to last," says the second.
"My blood is purer," says the third.
"I am more potent," says the fourth.
"I am more cataclysmic," says the fifth…
Their thirst doesn't seem to get quenched.

Antagonistic warriors
Coming with heavy artilleries
And smart drones to pound the bones
To wipe out all the facts
And block the living tracts.

The world is dying out
Disengaging the most devout
Going against nature
Looking past family and culture
Believing in all sorts of mysteries
Injustice bringing more miseries.

We must put an end
For the sake of earth's blend
Crying out in billions
For our Orchidaceae and reptilians
Breathing from our airway
And sharing the same DNA.

The Day I Die!

The day I die…

Streams shall run down
This aged mountain crown
With unobstructed density
Free from impurity.
A journey into the unknown.

Bells shall be echoing
Across the valleys narrowing
Accompanied with drums
Fortunate to hear some
Through the wide world spiralling.

My tears shall always be
Watering the small birch tree.
Another day shall come
Please do not succumb
To this pure source of glee.

Grieving my own death
When my very last breath
Meets the first afterlife
Drifting away from all strife
An epitaph with my body beneath.

Where shall I be
In a black or white sea?
The day I die
And my bones turn dry
Will I hear your goodbye?
Will I at last be free?

Macrocosm

A new era of crossing cultures
For the polyglot travellers
Awaiting to ravage the places.

A world open to us all
Like rats in a hole
Roaming the globe:

Drug culture
Trance music
Break beat techno
And free love

A humanitarian crisis applies
And symptoms stigmatise
For an early demise.

Artificial drugs
Psychoactive infesters
The toy of destinies.

Rising from coffins
Bodies and minds
In crazy hallucinations.

In trancelike stupors
Uttering bloopers
Catching other dupers.

Hitting the mainstream
Entering the bloodstream
Abolishing any dream.

The paraphernalia
Of fugues and hysteria
And deadly bacteria.

Artificial money
Sends cells into anergy
An unhinged lethargy.

Identity disorders rife
Triggered by digital life
The centre of strife.

Swimming in spermatozoids
Interacting with anthropoids
And spirits from other worlds.

What a grimy place
Of fats, sugar and spice
And a falsified paradise.

Lifeless seizures
Tasteless leisures
Craggy features.

Fake food
Fake happiness
In a fake world

Robbed of its riches
Causing illnesses
And scary alterations.

Sinking into apathy
And yet strangely
Ending tragically.

Let's forge human ties
Give, forgive and be wise
And strive for great moon rides.

Winter Nights

During long winter nights
Not much thrives when cold bites.

I cling to my blanket and lend an ear
Hoping this whole misery would soon retreat.

Wintery winds howling outside
Tossing my sanity to one side.

A thunderstorm takes matters to heights
Not sparing houses and streets of plights.

Discharging a lot of anger or revenge
Just about to throw me to the outer edge.

Striking once, twice, several times
The old power line nearby sparks.

From far distance come long rumbles
Sending loud, sharp, shooting crackles.

And high-pitched explosive sounds
Generate currents to deep grounds.

Creating sonic booms of shockwaves
Digging long and hard at our graves.

Out of life, out of touch, out of wire
And more chestnuts on the sizzling fire.

Stories of how our ancestors survived.
Untold riches which have long thrived but then died.

What is worse than a stormy night
Is knowing you will be all right.

Winter nights guarantee a total fright
Then the next day things will be yellow bright.

Two Worlds Apart

On our first encounter, it strikes
Our worlds are totally different.
Not as your gesture implies
That your feelings are constant.

"We were born from this breed
On a different planet to be.
Our roads have crossed indeed.
But you don't want to cross me."

"Most stars out there are shining bright
But yours is the only one tonight.
Open my heart and you shall see.
I am madly in love with thee."

And I truly and madly wish
Things would last a little longer.
When sands under your toes squish,
Your eyes become far more sombre.

Your eerie look will no longer deceive.
My stony face is harder to perceive.
Birds shall one day freely migrate
In pursuit of seasons and fate.

My Motto

I found the word
That would describe
My state of being:
'Unyielding'.

Taking a tumble
Every now and then
I walk and stumble
But move on again.

I weep when helpless
Energy boundless.
And burst with laughter
A cure thereafter.

Most lasting relationships
Cause daily pains and hardships
Like orchids flourish wildly
Then die unexpectedly.

Yet stronger than ever
Driven by endeavour
Immutable belief.
Washes away the grief.

Variations in alleles
Aid the wound as it heals.
Heels click when the heart's torn
Then a new me is born.

A messenger from heaven
Sending a divine weapon
To be as proud as a queen
For this is part of my gene.

Burrill Lake (Sydney)

The memories of that day on the lake path
Flash as I pray for rain to ease my wrath
Wiggling their way out along dusty lanes
To take me as far as horizon breaks.

"I 'mist' your shadow with all the wind's might
And take your pain away at the birds' flight.
Trust me, you'll feel a divine connection
Entrust me a part of your creation."

The spirits of deep serenity speak
Just as the lake wakes up from its calm sleep.
A million-and-a-thousand-year journey
Vivacious to last till eternity.

The morning sun covers its pewter skin
Revealing the rights of its next of kin.
Consumed by loving thoughts, life starts bustling
Inside and out my cranium is humming.

Magnificent Wild Rainbow Lorikeets
Come from everywhere to pastures to feed
On golden pollen and flower nectars
Or small fruit and seeds from passerby's hands.

After they fly out again into pairs
To their nesting areas in eucalypts
Chasing away predatory species
Mountainous and sea birds, even magpies.

Moody black swans are there also in queue
Paying their sincere homage and offering.
Watching them is *bona fide* blessing
With their graceful beauty as fresh as new.

Wombats emerge far from the waterfront
To be patted by the adventuresome.
Carrying their young in their belly pouch
Aggressive defenders known not to slouch.

With leaps and bounds of flora and fauna
Blood throbs in the veins of ballerinas.
A natural shrine in the Milky Way
Takes part in rehearsing a full ballet.

"I'm taken by the thought of certitude
You're inside me in times of solitude."
I whisper to it and burn as incense
In upturned roots of grand eucalyptus.

In the dark and frost of my solemn bed
The mist sways me over to the far lake.
Times of tenderness, times of affection
Times of fondness, times of absolution.

Aurelia

My head is slowly shutting down
Battery has gone willingly dead.
I need to puddle, to get brown
Elsewhere for my mind to be fed.

So close to Sydney harbour coasts
They venture out on the seashore
Seemingly looking like white ghosts
On a traveller's tale to explore.

Pink, white, lavender and orange
Waters have little oxygen.
Expanding in bays and harbours
Males and females are still toddlers.

Heading out on their adventures
They boot, jump, punt, dance and giggle.
Secretly mooring in shelters
Like stars of the ocean twinkle.

These translucent moonlike creatures
Under masses of cold waters
They drift with the currents as pros
Exploring caves, touching corals.

The not-so-long-ago blue sky
Instantly has patches of clouds.
A rough ocean and crackling sounds
Give the area enough supply.

Threatened, they have little motion.
Strikingly live through diffusion.
When hungry, they feed on plankton
Or touched, infect with their venom.

Haunted by other predators
Stinging them with their tentacles.
Moon jellyfish are petrified
Glowing, they're misidentified.

On a Cloud

As they sat on a cloud
Promises were bound.

"The next ring you'll wear
Comes from a love you won't bear."

What he described
Was what she desired.

And she closed her eyes
Wishing they weren't lies.

A painting so complete
Of words never to delete.

"You see, honey, nothing is permanent
For history has always been turbulent."

Although the storm is transient
Its eruption is indeed imminent.

Night clouds have no stem
As they travel on them.

And when clouds pour their rain
They're hurt and in pain.

Too weak to make a commitment
Too scared to lose the tournament

Somewhere their feet were shaky
A 12-week premature baby.

Rights and Obligations

Despite big things that concern you
Forever remember these two:

Rights and obligations
Versus dreams and aspirations.

Simple words that matter to me
To see you all right, my sweetie.

The truth is I know why rivers flow
Why chirping birds pack and go

Why the sun unshakeably rises
And the moon lights up the horizons

Why thunder happens with all its might
And eagles have passion for height

But in short, I do not understand
How feelings can easily change?

It is true they live in moments
Fighting hard their opponents

Yet as moments move
We also move in a groove.

Defect of History

History will never forgive
The killers of those who live.

There is no justification
For Ted Bundy's deep deviation

For Mikhael Popkov's, Luis Garavito's
Gary Ridgway's and Andrei Chikatilo's.

There is no reasonable excuse
For those who feed drug abuse.

For the ones who badly rule
And with hatred others fuel.

For names soft sciences give
To those who hold souls captive.

Feed them enough dope
To hang themselves on a rope.

Make them or break them
Who are you to condemn?

A man's pride is not fickle
It is worth more than a nickel.

On a Dream

Leaving early
On a rainy morning
I missed my plane.

Gathering myself
Outside doorsteps
Hoping their smell
Would remind me
Of my old house
So I find refuge.

Soft music
Flows sensitively
Through the half-closed window.

Failing to close
My chilled eyes
Searching for sleep
An evening

For a word
Unaffected by time.

Purple lines
In darkness
There in front of me.

Paintings
In my soul
Of numerous years
Speak now.

Stalled some place
Between the sky
And the earth

I am not evil
Yet I killed
Unwillingly.

This dream now
Does it belong
To this year
Or to a different year?
Of this century
Or of the last?

When you spoke
Words gushed out
Heavy and unclear.

Others wondered.
You and I
Only knew.

Coming across
Your photograph
A lunar halo
A statue
Of the inner self.

When you kiss me
I shall leave too.

I am shattered
Cannot recover.
Often I rest
In your quiet town

And dream
Of your hands
Warm in mine.

You have returned
To start with others.

How many secrets
Did you take with you?

A pile of bones
Broken
Unexpected visitors.

Condensed years
You have managed well
To distil my identity

Thank you
To geography
And its journeys…

My son
In our backyard

Moves a stick
From one spot to another

Inscribing
His own dreams
In two continents.

Holding me tight
He sits
On my lap
Complaining of his hunger
Then surprised
By his little finger
That reaches to my cheek
And wipes a tear.

My grey cat
Purrs beside my feet

An infant's voice
Screams
A few more words…

A mountain collapses
A whole world.

Appeared in The Geography of Memory, *Sydney,*
By the Ethnic Communities' Council of N.S.W. 1997.

Interference

We had a great olive tree
Growing on the side of the parking area
For over a century
Forming a boundary
For U-turns.

It shielded us in winter
And shaded us in summer.
Its branches gave us arms
To cuddle and rest
We knew how to find our way
Around them.
We grew accustomed
To each other.

One branch in particular
Became a lap.
Hours on hours
We'd play and dream
In the most important place
Of our fantasy land…

Years later, one morning
I look back at it
And all that is left sticking out
A stump.

"God damn it… Where is it?'
I yell at mom.

"What do you think?
It has never borne any fruit."
She laughs.

"But its value?"

My neck pulse throbs
And I flee to my room.

Suddenly, I was seven years old
Having no interest
In what's happening around me
Throwing myself into
The tree's arms
Holding on tight
As it tells me stories
Of the old days.

I thought of a hill
Down from our place
Where I embraced the dense
Oak bush with joy.

A brown patch grew slowly
Day by day
Until it ate
All of the mountain away.

The river turned muddy
Injecting the sea
For a few kilometres out.
From a distance
Exploitation has left nothing.
My pain grew unbearably.
Perhaps I had been wrong
To come back…

My great olive tree
No longer held the key
To my childhood.

That night, it stayed with me.
I swung my black curly hair about
Felt safe with it.
I did not want to let go.

Appeared in The Geography of Memory, *Sydney,*
By the Ethnic Communities' Council of N.S.W. 1997.

Takers in the Night
(Song)

Takers in the night!
Ripping souls apart
To never see the star
Leaving them confined
Dark injured minds.

Takers in the night!
Hiding in the rain
Screaming in deep pain
Playing their hard games
And casting their own flames.

Takers in the night!
Stealing the magic lights
Beating souls and hearts
Breathing their own greed
Behind bars, never to be freed.

Takers in the night!
Haunting darkened eyes
Evil in disguise
Marrying an angel
So life will be gainful.

Givers of the day!
Swing with the dance
Don't miss out your chance
Dawn will soon break out
Be ready for your flight.

Because You Are Beirut!

A mega-blast rips through the capital
Sending shock waves of thick ammonium taste
Bodies are buried under the rubble
And an entire area lays waste.

A cloud of death hovers yellow above
Tainted by burnt bodies, shipwrecks and stains
A torn city in search of the peace dove
Struggling to cope with its multiple strains

The thundering explosion is damn loud
Triggering tremor, disrupting the ground.
Districts are slit, streets bleed, people in fears
As the dead are mourned, the nation's in tears.

One of the oldest cities in the world
Inhabited five thousand years ago
A regional seaport anciently pearled
Your archaeological sites still glow.

Over the years they've tried to destroy you
Bring you down, conquer you or proclaim you.
Blast-torn, crisis-hit, corruption-dragged
Sung by some, cursed by others, terror-tagged.

Set ablaze, your heart rises from the flames
Searching for peace broken into pieces
For the countless souls that left before us
The sake of the dreams of those after us

We come to you in ache, yet not injured
Stripped of everything, yet barely naked
Lost in a sea of hatred, yet not drowned
Stabbed a thousand times a day, yet blended.

Angry, appalled, offended or wounded
We shall fight boldly for you all bonded.
In pain we unite, with joy we refuel
Because you are Beirut, a unique jewel.

(In tribute to the victims of Beirut explosion on August 4th, 2020)

A Margin of Peace
(65 Haiku Poems)

A silvery moon
Ascends behind the mountain
A sweet sensation.

Lulling me to sleep
The scent of honeysuckle
The last of the storm.

A white cloud of winter
Moves like a snake overhead
Welcoming summer.

On a dull fall day
The ticking of the hall clock
Awakens the birds.

Dry mountains await
The coming of spring flowers
Coloured lines and shades.

A wind approaches
Wrinkling the water surface
Down at the seashore.

In the deep blue sea
Fairy mermaids lure the ships
Power to cast spells.

Totally immersed
You've turned my world upside down.
Great Barrier Reef!

The crunch of gravel
Pierces right through to my bones
Drawing me awake.

Trees in the shadow
Surrounded by sands and hills
Appear unyielding.

The widow spider
Makes a silk thimble-shaped web
A great masterpiece.

People and shadows
Cross memory at light speed
Leaving me stranded.

A fire dances
Providing me with relief
In the still moon night.

Watching the dry fields
A gust of wind sweeps over
Right into my face.

Up in the thick hills
Flakes of drizzle calm the place
Before they feel me.

A flower withers
Touched by the frost of the night
A static relief.

Vertical fires
Consume my inner pieces
Burning themselves out.

Clouds from the unknown
Multiple shades of grey sky
Rather worrisome.

Birds of steel and stone
Dangle above dense cities
No place for shelter.

Coming and going
Deep misfortunes of the hearts
Break on fiery sand.

Trundling grizzly bears
Head to fast-moving rivers
Craving for fat fish.

Suggestive apples
Ignoring curious starers
Speak their sign language.

A frightened small bird
Guarding a warm branchy nest
A praying owl lands.

Valleys between us
Bridges about to crumple
Ripping us apart.

In deep sea waters
Darkness has no boundaries.
Life hardly exists.

Feeling out of place
Birds signal their departure
To nest someplace else.

A window is open
Fall breeze keeps chilling my skin
Sweeping the dry air.

Thoughts accelerate
Spreading over all the way
Intoxicated.

A duplicate heart
Behaving suspiciously
Finds nowhere to rest.

On a midmorning
Humid air embraces me
Sunshine of a day.

Lingering for days
Sheer illusions dissipate
Giving me some hope.

The mountain waits still
Toasting under the hot sun.
Snow will soon be here.

In the dark forest
The hoot of a nearby owl
Sounds so sorrowful.

Harsh and long winter
Only the tough trees survive
Days of denial.

Riding the high waves
A great white shark surges out
About to attack.

Seagulls caw and squawk
Fiercely on red summers
Looking for a bait.

Flames is all I feel
From fires eating my soul
Ash is what is left.

The rain is so near
Revealing its true dark side
Nightmares never end.

A bloody sunset
Forever the infinite
Blown into pieces.

People come and go
Wavy faces in the sea
Break from the mainstream.

Worse than anthracite
Hatred made of flame and smoke
Hypnotises me.

A familiar scent
Of a pine tree bush nearby
And ocean fragrance.

A tender morning
Pushes the mist down the cliffs
And cold disappears.

Refreshing and cool
Love is everlasting rain
Cleansing my deep wounds.

Ever-so gently
Fingers caress bare bodies
Two souls intertwined.

Same as human beings
The cosmos holds elements
Losing their ions.

I dance with the spumes
And the sounds of the ocean
Abundance of wealth.

Hovering above
Birds patrol a small area
My angel guardians.

On a high summit
Fluffy snow quietly falls
An eagle lands there.

Floating on the lake
Swans stretch their long gracious wings
A slow-motion flight.

In sun-baked valleys
Lies a craggy dying heart
Waiting for rescue.

Entering my sky
A meteorite's about
To touch my deep earth.

Taken by my thoughts
I drift away into space
Your voice is my way.

The forest's giants
On the side of the river
Guard the water path.

Just as desolate
Oak trees struggle with nature
Heavy, yet tender.

A unique journey
For my lonely heart to sing
On the edge of time.

Rushing all the way
Waves come and go on the shore
Another rebirth.

Time transmits its beams
A melodic lullaby
Echoes in the air.

Flowers in the wind
Their petals are blown away
Uniting tissues.

Thirsty plants and trees
Call upon the sky to weep
And submerge their fields.

On hot sweaty night
Memories are mixed with fun
And sweet illusions.

Despising daylight
Packs of wolves howl all night long
A full moon party.

Choppers overhead
Like itsy bitsy spiders
Want to weave their web

Leaves drop from branches
In a trembling departure
A short-lived journey.

Like a crowned statue
A dove holds an olive branch
A domed sepulchre.